LIFE OF ST. DUNSTAN

LIFE OF ST. DUNSTAN

BYRHTFERTH OF RAMSEY

Copyright 2024 by Dalcassian Press

All rights reserved. No part of this book may be reproduced in any manner whatsoever without written permission except in the case of brief quotations embodied in critical articles and reviews.

No part of this publication may be reproduced, distributed, or transmitted in any form or by any means, including photocopying, recording, or other electronic or mechanical methods, without the prior written permission of the publisher, except in the case of brief quotations embodied in critical reviews and certain other non-commercial uses permitted by copyright law. For permission request, write to Dalcassian Press at admin@thescriptoriumproject.com

Translator: Curtin, D.P. (1985-)

ISBN: 979-8-8692-1229-0 (Paperback)
ISBN: 979-8-8692-7421-2 (eBook)
Library of Congress Control Number:

Printed by Ingram Content Group, 1 Ingram Blvd, La Vergne, Tennessee
First Printing 2024, Dalcassian Press, Wilmington, DE

This work is part of a series produced in association with the Scriptorium Project and its community of scholars and translators.
Please visit our website at: www.thescriptoriumproject.com

INTRODUCTION

To the most prudent lord archon Alfric, chief of all priests, B. Bridfertus, a humble native of the Saxons, greetings of the highest joys of heaven.

1. Indeed, you, most exalted pastor, due to the enormity of your widely known expertise, and because of the magnificent and serene dignity of your privilege, I beseech you to grant me your unparalleled protection [before] all others, even though they are clear in doctrine, to receive the sacred task: I would attempt to extol the merits of the illustrious Dunstan with the eloquent pen of a suitable editor, unless the praises of his glorious life and the entire definition of this little work were to be sullied by a degenerate style of vices, as you can see. Therefore, I first confess this disgrace before all others with an open declaration to your serenity, and I, like the winged ones who seem to strike their wings before they utter the voice of departure, prostrate myself at your knees, releasing my burdens. Thus, I say, whatever you find in this edition that is used against the norm of the compositor's orthography, I urge you to command it to be corrected by imperial authority, and to amend it as a lamenting little feather of flowing ink is reformed from error. Moreover, I also encourage both orders of both sexes, who tread upon this slender harvest of our little book with the feet of letters, to do so with the full intent of their hearts, and rather with your support; but with caution, lest they carelessly trample upon the rare seeds of the germ; and in the meantime, while they strive to completely extirpate the vegetables sought in the depressed harvest, let them rather cut off just plantings, intercepted along with the evils, with a little hoe, uprooting them; but let the execrable darnel of this surface be expelled with a slight effort, scattered carelessly throughout the spaces of the places. If these preambles are to be granted to me… I will bring forth sufficiently gracious benefits; but if, however, they are scorned, rejected by the envious rival's accusations, it is cer-

tainly unknown what is better to begin, than to proceed with my own sickle, although it is ragged, covered with the mutilation of thinness, to atone for my own harvest of labor as much as I can: if, however, it is indicated by a certain demonstrative finger of the corrector in which part of the places I may fall provoked by the reproach of the vitiated field. Therefore, since ignorance will not allow me to do what I wish, I am compelled to do what I can. Indeed, as I had longed to mention the theologian in the desired preface (which I had wished to discuss with a pleasant eulogy of ease, or, if I could, to summarize, to treat the entire series of this texture with a golden scheme and the twofold resplendent color of electrum in gems), now at least I will proceed with satirical folly, stumbling as if less wise. However, I reserve the beauty of such a life to suitable composers (unless I fear the impending wrath of the blessed bishop); because I do not profess to be superior in any situation of this cosmos; but all persons, lacking the doctrine of the divine, are despised. For among the prudent, you hardly know anyone educated with a liberal mind, who seems to misuse such deformed eloquence in writing prologues, as I do. Nevertheless, these following pages, composed somewhat with a small spark of capacity, having been purged by the most faithful testimony of the faithful, if you distrust that I have preserved any insignia of my own temerity in these, unless perhaps those which I learned either by seeing or hearing, albeit with a dull intellect, from him himself; or even from his pupils, whom he led from tender youth to fully grown men, decently instructed in the fodder of doctrines, by educating them himself. I beseech you to accept, surrounded only by the bond of charity, this slender collection of these little points, hardly solidified by ebony title and dark style, to be defended against all envious rivals with invincible protection, not given to a petty rumor, but specifically granted to your sublimity. In this indeed literary plain, I request to explore a mind more spontaneous in its surroundings than the sluggish ignorance of its components: and I advise you, without causing you any annoyance, to be informed by the virtues of such a Father, to be instructed by his examples, to be fortified by his morals, to be justified by his disciplines:

so that, being his successor on earth, you may deserve to be his eternal confessor in heaven, through our Lord Jesus Christ, who with the coeternal Father and the Holy Spirit lives and reigns God, throughout all ages of ages. Amen.

1

CHAPTER ONE

Birth, education, studies, stay in the royal court, and expulsion from there.

2. As many periods had passed devoid of the true worship of the Christian religion, during which the people of England chose to be enslaved more by the ancient error of paganism than by Christ the Creator of all, the merciful Lord, lest His creation, ensnared by diabolical traps, perish damned forever, foresaw a remedy for eternal salvation from that blindness and, having compassion, sent the venerable Father Augustine, chosen by blessed Pope Gregory, to these parts of the homeland: who with the keen intellect of his mind converted the ignorant people of the faithful, uniting them as heirs in the blessed companionship of angels. Therefore, as soon as the man of God had sown the furrow of the most renowned doctrine among the thorns of the ignorant nation and had planted the wheat seed of the Holy Trinity, he uprooted the viperous germ of the perishing darnel, so that henceforth the overgrown ruins of the wild countryside would not sprout in it, and he demonstrated that worthy fruits of repentance should be offered to God both by teaching and example. Thus, the entire people of Albion, who had previously scorned it, believed in the Lord and were joined to their God through the recognition of true faith. More-

over, without whose care even little sparrows do not fall, he then took care of the best provision for their condition. For he chose nourishing kings, bishops, dukes, deans, provosts, and the other rulers of his Church from those who would come to him, to govern the flock reborn to God under the protection of peace with justice after each had completed their own space.

3. Among these principal men of royal preeminence, whom many most Christian and orthodox rulers had preceded in reign, whose names now the difficulty does not allow to be examined individually, the glorious King Aethelstan is numbered among the kings of the Angles in the succeeding years. During the times of this reign, a vigorous boy arises in the borders of the West Saxons: whose father is called Heorstan, and his mother is named Cynedrydis. His pious parents, having him reborn in the waters of sacred baptism, named him Dunstan. Thus the boy grew and became dear both to God and to men. There was a certain royal island at the border of the aforementioned man, now called Glastonbury by the ancient name of the neighbors, measured by wide bays of places, surrounded by fish-filled waters and stagnant rivers, and suitable for many human needs, and (which is the greatest) dedicated to the gifts of God. Indeed, in this place, the neophytes of the first Catholic law found an ancient church, not constructed by the art of men, but rather prepared for human salvation by heavenly means: which afterwards the Creator of heaven demonstrated would be consecrated to Himself and to His holy mother Mary, through many miraculous deeds and various virtues of mysteries. They also added another stone oratory, which they dedicated to Christ and His apostle St. Peter. Furthermore, thereafter the frequency of all the faithful gathered around, and they humbly frequented the precious place of the said island. Therefore, it happened that for such causes, the aforementioned man Heorstan, accompanied by the blessed boy Dunstan, passed through Glastonbury, and while they were staying there for the purpose of prayer, behold, a sweet sleep

covered the boy, and he saw in an excess of his mind a certain old man clothed in snowy whiteness, leading him through the pleasant atriums of the sacred temple, and showing him the monastic buildings, which were to be built after his pastoral care, in the order in which they are now reported to be established.

4. Afterward, the religious parents of the boy Dunstan committed him to the sacred leisure of letters: to whom the Lord immediately deemed it worthy to confer such grace of His bounty, that he surpassed all his contemporaries and easily surpassed the times of his studies:

> *But what the highest Majesty had granted him as a sign,*
> *In studies themselves, I shall reveal as best I can.*
> *It happened that he labored long, for he was afflicted by severe fevers,*
> *So much so that he suffered from a bitter madness,*
> *Unmindful and lost in delirium,*
> *He cast forth many words empty from his mouth.*
> *Worn down by these calamities, he was entrusted to a certain woman,*
> *Who at that time would care for the tender pupil,*
> *And took care under her that he would not perish from the plague.*
> *But the mentioned plague pressed heavily upon the boy,*
> *So that he lay as if lifeless, stretched out to the end.*
> *His whole body became as if he were already about to die.*
> *And when he was thus burdened for a long time by the weight of evil;*
> *Behold, suddenly he moved, and quickly rose again,*
> *He seized a stick and a little branch that he happened to find;*
> *With which, striking the air on both sides,*
> *As if he were defending himself from rabid dogs, he went.*

Thus also, it is said that at night he hastened to the very peribola of the temple

> *As a solitary, and from there came to the high*

Ascents of the steps, where the craftsmen of works were accustomed to climb,
Who, with great danger,
Alas, timid ones! wove the tops of the temple.
There, as a strong man, he ascended to the highest citadel,
And too carelessly stood upon it and swayed.
But the mercy of the Lord snatched him from the heights
Of the innocent from the falls; also placing him down
Unharmed in body, safe and sound,
Inside this very temple, carried down from the summit;
Where two guardians were lying together as was customary,
So that the third might rest among them.
He, however, did not know by what means he would come,
To devise a way, living under the heavens.
For the doors of the temple were not opened to anyone going in,
But the same iron was barred under the hard bark.
Now, best reader, confess in swift speech,
What seems to you to be true in this small matter:
If you doubt such a one to ascend the temple of the heavens;
Who is enclosed in the temple with closed doors for the salvation of ruin,
Is established in the temple, (so) that he may redeem from the evil stain
Afterwards, through many, and send forth to the heavens troops,
Distributing doctrines, and also leaving examples.
Let the humble patient arise, let the proud fall.

For the more he was growing taller, the more he was enriched in the sharpness of intellect; and the more matured by the rolling years, the more fervent in God's love; and the more accustomed in divine praises, the more insistent in his persevering spirit.

5. Therefore, the aforementioned parents, seeing the great excellence of their son, deemed it worthy to impose upon him the clerical office and associated him with the famous monastery of Glastonbury;

so that he might serve God and the Mother of God, Mary, there day and night, continuously. Now, being bound by divine disciplines, he trampled upon the years of his flourishing youth, having overcome his adolescence: and just as the cedar of Lebanon, he flourished with the vigor of virtues in the house of his God: and planted in the divine courts, he extended the strength of his growth towards the heavens each day. Meanwhile, the fame of his great constancy became known in the king's palace, so that it was widely disseminated through magnificent testimonies of praiseworthy deeds. However, he was not seeking the vain favors of this world, but was endowed with the riches of virtues, carrying within him the glory of the eternal King, which was dictated to him by powerful wisdom, by the learned finger of spiritual gifts, by the variety of studies, and by the shining brilliance of golden adornments. For he flew through many meadows of sacred and divine volumes, like a clever bee, with such rapidity of a capacious mind, that he nourished his mind rather than his body with divine readings, and his pure heart, infused with the breath of the Holy Spirit, devoutly supplied the sense with a honeyed taste. Furthermore, the pilgrims from Ireland cherished the place I mentioned, Glastonbury, as well as the other crowds of the faithful, especially in honor of Blessed Patrick the Younger, who is said to have peacefully rested there in the Lord. He also diligently cultivated the writings of those who philosophized about the path of true faith, and of other wise men, whom he perceived to be solidly established by the assertions of the holy Fathers from the innermost perspective of the heart, and he always investigated with a resolute inquiry. Thus, he constrained the study of his life, so that whenever he scrutinized the books of divine Scripture, God seemed to speak with him; and whenever, freed from worldly cares, he was soothed by the leisure of prayers, he appeared to converse equally with the Lord.

6. Therefore, while these exercises of good works were being carried out, some of his own companions and court officials, especially

those of his own blood, who envied his salutary deeds, attempted to gnaw or cut off the vine and branch of the holy vine, which was striving for the heavenly kingdoms, namely the blessed Dunstan, flourishing in Christ, with the sharp tongues of serpents and the dreadful bites of dire teeth, like the bristly goat. For they were kindling an unexpected scab of deceit against him under the lurid cave of their blemished hearts, saying that he had learned from salutary books and skilled men, not for the salvation of souls, but the most vain songs of ancestral paganism, and that he cultivated the frivolous chants of enchantments in histories. To this disease of deceit, the blessed novice always opposed Christ, who knows all things before they come to be: in whose person the kind prophet David, and his most faithful witness, forewarned by the oracle of the Holy Spirit, thus spoke concerning false authors of the Lord's passion: "Witnesses of iniquity have risen up against me, and iniquity has lied to itself" (Psalm XXVI, 12). And again: "Those who sought evil against me spoke vanities, and all day long they meditated on deceit" (Psalm XXXVII, 13). And the Lord Himself said in the Gospel: "Blessed are you when men hate you, etc." (Luke VI, 22), and to his listeners: "If you were of the world, the world would love its own; but because you are not of the world, but I chose you out of the world, therefore the world hates you" (John XV, 19). Also: "Blessed are you when men revile you and persecute you, and say all evil against you falsely for my sake. Rejoice in that day and be exceedingly glad, for great is your reward in heaven" (Matthew V, 11). Therefore, the servant of God Dunstan, strengthened by the firmest pledge, became like a deaf man, not caring for the voice of rebuke, as he hardly ever opened his mouth against the dogs barking at him through the bitter eloquence of reproach. They, however, persisting in their wicked machinations, falsely accused him before the king, and obtained that he be expelled from their company: whom, if they had been of sound mind, they would have loved uniquely. Then, with the most atrocious rage of impiety prevailing, seizing the innocent man with their fourfold limbs, like a patient sheep, bound by hands and feet, they threw him into the muddy places of the marshes: and to make him more contemptible in their madness, they trampled on him with their feet, until, according to the malice of their will, they dishonored him in the stinking mire. But when they departed, he scarcely rose from the muddy river, as if beaten down: and he decided to come to a certain friend, distant a mile from there, to wash himself there. But there met him the same fierce dogs: and since he was disfigured by mud, they thought him more a monster than a man, and with cruel barking they attacked him: however, as they heard the voice of one soothing, they soon recognized him, only by his silence. Then he, groaning from the depth of his heart, said: "O savage madness of my relatives, changed from human affection to canine cruelty! For the irrational nature of dogs has shown me affection with a wagging tail: but the kinship of humanity, forgotten, has instilled the severity of the dogs that harass me; thus the wicked order of both has changed the just way in both."

2

CHAPTER TWO

The Monastic Life of St. Dunstan. The deeds and pious death of Aethelfleda the widow. An antiphon from the harp.

7. Therefore, the ancestral enemy of the human race, realizing the aforementioned youth, through the sinister messengers of envious companions whom he had sent, found that he had yielded little to their wicked wills, with which they began to fight against him with arms; but how great struggles of temptations he inflicted upon himself, the following page of this little book will partly reveal. For first, he cast upon him the love of women, by which, through the embraces of familiar women, he might delight in worldly pleasures. Meanwhile, his relative Elphegus, surnamed the Bald, a faithful prelate, earnestly requested him with many petitions and spiritual admonitions to become a monk. But he, renouncing the instigation of the aforementioned deceiver, preferred to court a young girl, whose daily flatteries he enjoyed, rather than to be clothed in the monastic habit of sheep's wool. But when the man of God heard the words of refusal, he soon from the depths of his heart sighed and sought the ruler of the heavenly kingdoms, that He might bring him the judgments of his corrections, so that he who scorned His admonitions might recognize them sharply: which, with God's mercy favoring, is proven to have been ac-

complished in a short space of time. For in that way, the intolerable pain of swelling bladders enveloped his whole body, so that he thought he was suffering from the disease of an elephant, and had no hope for his own life. Then, hastily, seized by great anguish, he sent for the bishop, whom he had already previously scorned, and called him with a humble plea, announcing that he wished to obey his salutary admonitions: and he, coming to visit him, consecrated him as a consoled and amended monk of God.

8. Therefore, the pious and merciful Lord, having compassion on His servant Dunstan, withdrew him from the love of women: who (as history relates) called back John the Apostle and Evangelist, especially beloved by Him, from the marriage bed. Thus, with this correction from God and the salutary teaching of the blessed bishop Elphege, the effect of love was understood, and sometimes after the kindness of the same pontiff, for the sake of the most beneficial doctrine and kinship, he diligently adhered with continuation. Meanwhile, the religious citizens of Winchester invited the same pontiff of God to the dedication of a new church, which they had built in their city of Winchester, where he held the governance of the bishopric, for the reverence of the supreme Deity, in the southern part of the popular street, which is now said to be closer to all the churches on the western side. Among others, Dunstan was present at this consecration, being one of the foremost. When it was dedicated, they gathered the venerable man with his companions for the prepared feasts of charity, celebrating a joyful day in honor of such a man and for the celebration of the consecration. However, after giving thanks, as night was approaching, the pontiff rose and, having blessed those dining, both men and women, returned to his own; and they went along the way to the church consecrated to St. Gregory the Pope; and there, stopping, the bishop said to Blessed Dunstan: Let us complete our evening office here at the oratory of our holy Father Gregory. And they approached, after the voices of prayers, joining their heads together as usual, so that their

confessions might mutually benefit one another. When this was done, while the bishop was granting the remission of sins, a huge stone fell from the high air, and, by the mercy of the Lord, it fell to the ground between both heads with a violent crash; touching only the hair of each head, it harmed none of them; which, if I am not mistaken, that wicked one, the enemy of every righteous work, cast down from his darts of wickedness, as if he were to avenge a double wrath on both.

9. At that time, it happened that a certain deacon of the Church of Glastonbury, named Wulfred, underwent temporal death: who, while he lived, was both a prelate and a familiar friend to Blessed Dunstan. Therefore, not long after his departure, he appeared to him rejoicing, revealing many unknown things about the heavens, moreover defining the whole course of his life, and the fates of his future age and events of good and evil. When the blessed man heard such lights of mysteries and such inevitable occurrences of his life, he said, in a state of mental exaltation: If what you affirm is true and to be believed, how shall I know? By what signs will those things be made clear to me? But he led him into the courtyard of the temple, where the bodies of the deceased rest, and with his finger pointed to a spot in the southern part of the church that was unshaken, and said: Because what I have told you is true, know for certain that in this place, three days ago, a certain priest was to be buried, and he is not yet weak; however, his little body will be carried for burial from the western part of the present temple. At this voice of vision, the blessed Dunstan, awakened, after the first hour of the day, came with some to the aforementioned spiritual cemetery, and also taking a small stone that could be thrown, he threw it at the spot, adding this: If what I saw in my dreams is true, a certain priest must be buried here three days before. Furthermore, as they were departing, the master and priest of a certain Aethelfleda, a most noble and most religious matron, came with another company of companions, and obtained the same place for burial among some eloquent words, saying: When I am dead, I pray, bury me here. Indeed, he

was still healthy according to the testimony of many; but when they had departed a little from there, he was burdened with a serious illness near the end of his life. Then, on the following night, he commended his last spirit to Christ the Lord, and was buried three days later in the very place of his choice, which had been assigned to Blessed Dunstan before.

10. Now I gradually interrupt the conversation by delaying it, until I shall present some brief words, which I do not consider should be omitted, with a little eloquence. For there was a certain very wealthy matron, born of royal lineage, but bound by the strict ties of divine religion, whose name we have recently touched upon in brief mention. After losing her husband, desiring to lead a widow's life according to the quality of her strength, she decided to establish small dwellings for herself in the kinship of the sacred temple on the western side, so that for the desire of the heavenly kingdom, she would not cease to serve the Lord Jesus Christ there day and night. To her, the blessed Dunstan always adhered, who loved her in a way that was remarkable above all others; and for the sake of religion and also of kinship, he diligently relieved her poverty. However, it is not within our capability to recount in detail the eloquence of words how she prepared herself for divine services. Nevertheless, the Lord, the inspector of all secrets, declared what merit she had, both in the last times of her life and also while she lived in this world. Therefore, she loved all royal seed, from which she derived the origin of her nobility, with an intimate fervor of charity; and thus she often served kings with the grace of sweetness from her own possessions. From this pious custom, she prepared a meal for the glorious King Aethelstan, as best she could, because she foresaw that he had come to Glastonbury for the sake of prayers. Knowing that the royal attendants had been promised by the king to divert to him, they came the day before to see if all the necessary provisions were available or suitable. And upon seeing everything, they said to her: You have sufficient supply for all the service, if the liquor of mead does not

fail you. But she replied: May my lady, the holy Mother of my Lord Jesus Christ, not allow that anything in royal dignity should be lacking for me. And saying this, she quickly entered the ancient church of Mary, the Mother of God, and prostrated herself there to pray, long beseeching the most abundant support from the heavenly King, to increase the service for the king. What then? The king came, surrounded by a great company at the appointed time; and after the celebration of prayers and masses, he joyfully entered for the meal. And indeed, at the first serving, they emptied that vessel of mead, to the measure of a single palm's breadth; and thus afterwards, with God increasing and the blessed matron deserving, nothing diminished, they remained, as is customary in royal banquets, pouring from horns and other vessels of indiscriminate quantity throughout the day. When the king himself heard of this marvelous deed from the accounts of the attendants, he said, his mind changed, to his own: We have sinned, burdening this servant of God with the excess of our multitude. And rising, after greeting his niece, he took his leave.

11. However, this servant of God, after completing the blessed contest, began to seriously weaken due to human law as the end approached: to whom Blessed Dunstan showed a clever reason for providing care, and he uniquely protected her as if she were his own mother. Therefore, with these cares hindering him, he was absent during the evening hours and was not with the usual crowds singing: yet at the twilight of the finished day, as he was going to the already observed church to complete the delayed office with the following scholars, while standing outside the church door for the sake of singing, he saw from afar a snow-white dove emerging from the eastern heavens, shining with wonderful beauty and a new appearance. Indeed, the tips of its wings resembled sparkling fire, and with lightning-like wings it scattered through the air: which swiftly flew to the chambers of the blessed matron. But Blessed Dunstan, not forgetting his sick friend, immediately returned after completing the psalms, and coming in,

heard her speaking within her veils with serious words, as if conversing with a certain familiar friend, exchanging words. He approached the confident maidservants observing their mistress, and wondering with whom she was speaking, he asked. But they said they did not know; but they said: Before you came, they said, the light of immense splendor filled this whole room with its brightness; and afterwards, when the light ceased, she (as you now hear) did not cease to speak to the one speaking. Then indeed he gradually sat down watching, until she somehow ceased from her speech. And while she had also ceased from speaking, he soon entered to her, casting aside the folds of her veils, and familiarly asked her with whom she was speaking. But she said to him: You also saw him coming before you came here, and now you ask with whom I have spoken? For he was speaking with me, who appeared to you while you stood before the church door singing: who also just now announced to me the entire course of my departure in order. Nevertheless, it is not very necessary for you, my friends, to be greatly saddened about me, for the mercy of my God will meet me as I die, and will allow me to enter the joys of paradise mercifully. But to you, as a special friend's minister, I impose this task that you too prepare for me early in the morning to hasten my baths, and to prepare the funeral garments which I shall wear, and after the washing of the body to celebrate the masses, and soon at the time of participation in the sacred blood and body of our Lord Jesus Christ to receive communion, so that thus at the same moment, led by the Lord, I may walk the way of the whole nation. This he most earnestly fulfilled, being a parent in all the commands of the blessed matron, so that he would not commit the final watch of his foresight, submitted to weariness of delay, to the torpid care. But she also most certainly fulfilled what had been shown to her about herself that night on this day in the order she had predicted; so that after the mystery of the mass, after the most healthful taste of the Eucharist, she likewise ended her life happily in the Lord Jesus Christ with the finished mass. Then the joyful overseer committed her soul to the Lord with a near fate, burying the body with honor, and gave her to the saints, as she herself had wished while she lived in the body. But the liberated attendant departed, wishing that this might rest in the sweetness of the Lord.

12. Here also, among the sacred studies of literature, so that he might be suitable in all things, he diligently cultivated the art of writing, as well as the skill of playing the harp and painting, and, so to speak, shone as a vigilant inspector of all utensils. Wherefore, a certain noble matron named Aedelpyrm called him to her for a moment with a familiar prayer, so that he might prepare for her a certain stole for divine worship with various patterns, which later could be adorned with gold and gems. When he had done this upon coming, he took his harp with him, which we call a harp in the native tongue, so that he might delight himself at times with it and with those tending toward him. Then indeed, on a certain day after dinner, while both he and the aforementioned matron were returning to repeated works with their workers, it happened marvelously that the very harp of the blessed youth, hanging on the wall of the chamber, spontaneously sounded a joyful melody aloud without anyone touching it, to the ears of all. For it sounded the melody of this antiphon, and singing to the end brought it to completion: The souls of the saints who have followed the footsteps of Christ rejoice in heaven; and because they have shed their blood for his love, therefore they will reign with Christ forever. When they heard this, both he and the aforementioned matron, and all her workers, terrified, forgetting entirely the works in their hands, looked at each other astonished, greatly wondering what this marvelous event might prefigure as a new example.

3

CHAPTER THREE

Events under King Edmund. The Abbey of Glastonbury received; the snares of demons avoided.

13. Then, after the death of King Aethelstan, and the change in the state of the kingdom, the elevation of the succeeding king, namely Edmund, commanded B. Dunstan, who had been a man of good life and learned in language, to be present at his views, so that he too might be counted among the royal nobles and court princes. He, not rashly resisting these commands, but rather remembering the Lord's precept, which says to render to the king what is the king's, and to God what is God's (Matt. XXII, 21). Similarly, urged by the admonition of St. James the Apostle, he did not cease to submit himself to all human creatures, especially to those in power, whether to the king as the preeminent one, or to the leaders as sent by him, for the punishment of evildoers, but for the praise of the good, etc. (1 Pet. II, 13). Nor indeed, if I am not mistaken, did he forget the words of St. Paul the Apostle, who says: Let every soul be subject to the higher powers: for there is no power but of God: the powers that be are ordained of God; whosoever therefore resists the power, resists the ordinance of God; and they that resist shall receive to themselves damnation (Prov. XIII, 1). And again: Render therefore to all their dues; tribute to whom tribute is due;

custom to whom custom; fear to whom fear; honor to whom honor (Ibid., 7); and also to this same Apostle, in his own election, the Lord said: It is hard for you to kick against the pricks of my power (Acts IX, 5). For B. Dunstan diligently hid these and similar precepts of sacred Scripture in the depths of his heart, lest he should sin against the Lord; but he arranged the words of his commandments, sweeter than honey and the honeycomb (Ps. XVIII, 11), as a lamp for his feet, by which he might walk in the ways of the Lord. And after he had recognized himself as more earnestly taught or enlightened by the commandments of God, he swore with himself and firmly resolved in the secrets of his heart to keep, to the end, the judgments of his justice, so that the same Lord might say elsewhere regarding this same sentiment: He that endures to the end shall be saved (Matt. X, 22). And again: Be faithful unto death, and I will give you a crown of life (Rev. II, 10). Thus, although laboriously, he long dwelled with the high ones in the royal palace, holding the two reins of sacred governance, namely of the law and of theoretical as well as practical life. However, some of the soldiers residing there, seeing this constancy of his conduct, began to love him with the unique sweetness of charity or the love of kinship. On the contrary, many, shrouded in cloudy minds, began to detest the same man of God with the most bitter hatred of vanity, and to envy his prosperity even to death. These indeed, the accursed ones, for the increase of their wickedness, demanded that anyone else they could find pursue the servant of God. For they twisted the cord of their iniquity around him for so long, rather ensnaring themselves in it than him, so as to infect the king with their vices and make the credulous fall for their deceptions: who, immediately, as he had been instructed by the wicked before, moved with great fury, commanded that he, stripped of dignity, be deprived of all honor, and that he should seek out where he wished, without him and his own. There were, however, at Ceodri, where these things had happened, venerable men, namely messengers of the kingdom of the East, then staying with the king: whom he, as if already appointed to exile, began to pursue another plan, praying that they would not abandon him, left by the king, but would lead him back to his homeland, even to a place of residence. But they, feeling compassion for his sorrow, promised him all the comforts of his kingdom, if he would go with them.

14. Therefore, the king soon on another day, when he was to enjoy himself with his companions in the usual manner with hunting, and while they arrived at the woods to hunt, they eagerly took different paths of the wooded trails. And behold, from the various sounds of the cawing of crows and the barking of dogs, many deer took to flight: among them the king alone with a pack of dogs caught one to hunt: and he wore it down for a long time through various winding paths with the agility of his horse and the pursuit of the dogs. There is, however, in the nearby woods of Ceoddis, a certain precipice of a mountain cut off among many others, indeed remarkable and immensely deep: to which the same deer, I know not how, except by God's hidden will, fled and came; and he threw himself headlong into the depths of the same precipice along with the following dogs, and they all fell together, crushed to death. Similarly, the king, following the deer and the dogs, came with the great momentum of a flying horse, and immediately upon seeing the precipice, he tried to slow the course of the galloping horse as much as he could with his strength. But since he had a stubborn and rigid neck, he could not. In short, with all hope of his life taken away, he commended his soul into the hands of his God, yet saying within himself: I thank you, Most High, that I do not remember having harmed anyone these days, except only Dunstan: and this I will amend with a willing heart and preserved life reconciled to myself. At this statement, by the merits of the blessed man, the horse (which I now hesitate to say) stopped on the very edge of the precipice, where the front feet of his horse were almost about to plunge into the depths. Then he gave the greatest thanks and praises to God for the restoration of his life with both heart and mouth, clearly understanding with himself, and often rewarding in the secrets of his heart, that he was

nearly destined for the vengeance of such a great man's death; and coming home, he ordered that blessed Dunstan be summoned with great haste. When he had come at the call, the king said to him: Hurry as quickly as you can to prepare a horse for yourself, so that you can go with me with a small company where I am going. And immediately, having mounted their horses, they took the road that leads directly to Glastonbury; and when they arrived there, they entered the churches of God, as was fitting, to pray. And immediately, after their prayers were fulfilled and their eyes cleared from the streams of tears, the king again called to him the servant of God Dunstan; and taking his right hand, he kissed him for the sake of reconciliation or even dignity, and leading him to the priestly chair, he placed him in it, saying: Be a powerful prince and a faithful abbot of this seat, and whatever may be lacking to you from your own resources for the increase of divine worship or for the supplement of the sacred rule, I will devote to supply it with royal generosity.

15. Therefore, after this, the servant of God Dunstan, by the command of the king, received the aforementioned dignity for the sake of governance: and following the most salutary institution of St. Benedict in this manner, he shone as the first abbot of the English nation: thus he devoted himself to render spontaneous service to God from the affection of his heart. Then, therefore, the very prudent shepherd first firmly fortified the enclosures of the cloisters with monastic buildings and other fortifications, as had been indicated to him long ago by a certain elder through revelation, where he might enclose the Lord's sheep, gathered together far and wide, lest they be torn apart by the invisible wolf. Then, the same teacher of God began to nurture the gathered community entrusted to him with the divine word, and to drink from the heavenly source, namely from the honeyed document of sacred Scripture, teaching that through the narrow paths of this life one must pass to the eternal delights of heavenly feasts. For it is evident to almost all the faithful surrounding him, that, after a few years'

interval, the disciples whom he had tenderly inserted into the vine of true faith, namely Christ and the Lord, were growing abundantly, and were bearing the fruit of good works with obedient beauty. And after this, many pastors of the Churches, instructed by his teachings and examples, were sought to various cities or other holy places, chosen to be imbued there with sacred governance and the norms of justice, namely prelates, deans, abbots, bishops, even archbishops, the most distinguished from other orders. And whoever, however, from his disciples, having been untied by bodily bonds during those same times, met an inevitable death, undoubtedly sought the joys of heaven afar.

16. And when the ancient adversary, with a discerning mind, discovered that the blessed Father, indeed Dunstan, had snatched such great multitudes from his hands by plundering, he did not cease day and night to oppose him by whatever fraud he could. For one night, while the athlete of God was steadfastly occupied within the cloister's enclosure with psalms and vigils, the enemy of God and man appeared to him, bristly and terrifying in the form of a bear, wishing to frighten him in some way with a grim imagination and to somewhat dissociate him from an undertaking quite contrary to his purpose. But when the athlete of God perceived this hostile monster with a spiritual rather than a bodily gaze, he remained more secure in his praises of God, like an unconquered man. Afterwards, after a brief moment, the enemy appeared to him again, not in the form of the previous mockery, but in a canine form quite fitting for him, as are all his wicked deceits; so that he might deceive him with a feigned savagery of dogs and, by whatever means he could, separate him from the study of prayer. Nevertheless, that tenacious tempter raged in vain against the servant of God with his nefarious cunning: he proved to be supported on all sides by the arms of faith; and therefore, struck down by the aforementioned point of the holy cross, which he always carried in his right hand, he was annihilated. Yet he remained undaunted in the praise of Christ, disregarding the temptations of the adversary. The

same treacherous dragon also added, in a serpentine manner, to slither a third time, testing whether he might still find the man of God in a state of relaxed spirit to conquer: and then, indeed, from the wicked composition of his heart, he transformed himself into a foul little fox, so that even in this way he might divert the servant of God with a tail wagging and various antics from the intention of his God. When the blessed Father Dunstan had seen him transformed so many times, he smiled and said to him: "Go now, enemy, for you have now appeared sufficiently like yourself," and having made the sign of the cross, the enemy disappeared.

17. With these and such ghostly arms, the ancient seducer often tired the blessed Father Dunstan, albeit in a futile conflict: as also at one time, while he was laboring vigilantly in the work of prayer before the altar of Christ's martyr George. It is unknown by what circumstance, whether from the injection of the aforementioned deceiver or from the continuation of the vigils, a gentle sleep suddenly crept upon him while he was singing the words of the psalm: and it seemed to him, not, so to speak, entirely asleep, that a bristly bear, huge and terrible, was coming with great force, and was placing horrendous feet, prepared to tear him apart, upon both his shoulders, also standing over him with a greedy yawn, as if to devour him. And when the man of God awoke completely from the terror inflicted, he quickly seized the staff he always carried in his hand, striving to strike the nefarious monster with human fury: however, with a superfluous blow, he struck the wall of the temple, producing a great noise throughout the temple for all to hear. He himself, returning to himself, entered into a stronger combat of battle, namely by chanting this psalm of sacred contest: "Let God arise, and let His enemies be scattered" (Ps. LXVII, 3), as above; for in that place, overcome by sleep, he had abandoned the study of singing, and immediately, as they say, upon resuming this psalmody, that nebulous deceiver was recognized, like a very dark shadow, confused, and departed from the aforementioned form.

18. For there was a certain brother of this same man of God, named Wulfric, who was appointed as a powerful overseer in the affairs of his villages, so that neither he nor anyone from the monastic profession would wander outside, engaging in the trivialities of secular matters. This man, having completed his allotted time, was overtaken by a lethal condition and was about to face temporal death. For this reason, it happened that all the monks of the aforementioned temple went out for his funeral; and none remained at home except for the abbot and a small scholar (who later became a bishop and informed us of these events), so that they could carry the lifeless body to the monastery where it was to be buried with the sacred rites. Meanwhile, the abbot was walking with the same scholar to see (as I suppose) if the brothers had approached the deceased's body. And while he was always singing as was customary, a certain missile stone suddenly came flying over the old church, attempting violently to strike the head of the blessed Father; but, with God defending, it could not. Nevertheless, it struck the cap that covered his head, casting it far away as if it had been cut off by a pole. Turning to the scholar who was walking with him, he said: "Hurry, and take this movable stone as quickly as possible, so that you can bring it to me to see." When he, lifting it with great difficulty at the command of the Father, said, the venerable Father Dunstan replied: "O opposing enemy! You have long been preparing this blow of this stone against me with malicious intent." For, according to the testimony of many, there was no stone of such size, whether large or small, in the borders of Somerset, except perhaps in some stone works: and therefore it was evident from whose wicked hand it had sprung forth. Nevertheless, after this, he commanded that the stone, although it had been sent for his detriment, be kept in custody as a testimony.

4

CHAPTER FOUR

*E*vents under Kings Eadred and Edward. The episcopate refused. Exile.

19. Therefore, after King Eadmund was slain by the wicked thief, the next heir, namely Eadred, succeeded to the natural kingdom of his brother. Thus, strengthened in exaltation, he loved the blessed Father Dunstan with such fervor of charity that he hardly preferred anyone above him in primacy. On the other hand, the man of God, in order to repay the love he received from the depths of his heart, called him king, whom he held most dear by his usual appellation. From this confidence of charity, the king entrusted to him all the best of his belongings, namely many rural charters, even the ancient treasures of preceding kings, as well as various treasures of his own acquisition, to be faithfully kept under the protection of his monastery. And while, after some time, the fortunate man, the aged Aethelgar, bishop of the Church of Chrydion, was compelled by carnal law to end his life in Christ, the aforementioned king persuaded the man of God Dunstan with frequent exhortations to undertake the episcopate, now deprived of a father, under pastoral care. But he immediately rejected the excuse of the word, saying that he was not suited for such pastoral oversight, nor was he yet worthy of such a great dignity, by which he could keep so wide a fold of Christ with probable caution without his own

ruin. He sometimes opposed these and similar words of contradiction to the king until he completely suppressed all his persuasion by utterly refusing. Nevertheless, he was not able to change the secret intention of his will; for he desired that the one he loved more than the others should be elevated to a higher excellence. Therefore, he placed the words of his will in the mouth of his own mother, saying to her: "I wish, O my most beloved mother, that you have our special friend Dunstan invited with you at your dinner time, and while you enjoy pleasant conversations at the joyful banquet, strive to encourage him with feminine eloquence, so that he may become the bishop of the recently widowed Church according to our suggestion." When she had done this with all her efforts, she could not change him from his former declaration. However, by the counsel of Aelfwold, the venerable man, due to his powerful beauty, he was chosen for the same episcopate.

20. On the following night, it seemed to him through a nocturnal revelation that he should hasten to Rome with a ready company. Peter and Paul appeared to him on the same roads with Andrew, revealing to him various and unexpected secrets of their events: and when the familiar conversation with the apostles was finished, Andrew struck him with the rod he was holding, not with a slight blow, saying: "Take this as a reward for the delay you caused yesterday by refusing the fellowship of our apostleship." Immediately, after the words were spoken, he awoke and asked the monk lying before him who had struck him with the sharp blow of the rod. But he said: "No one, I say, has touched you while you were resting with any blow, to my knowledge." Therefore, he, having premeditated, said: "Now, my son, I know, now I recognize from whom I was struck." And, alas! it was King Eadred, beloved of Dunstan, who, throughout the time of his reign, was exceedingly languishing, so that during the time of refreshment, having taken the juice of food, he had rejected the remaining part, slightly chewed, from his mouth, and thus often caused a stinking nausea to

the soldiers dining with him by spitting it out. Although he was dragging out a sickly life in a decaying body for some time, the increasing languor, often invading him with a thousand weights, miserably brought him to his death. Then, from long sickness, uncertain of his own life, he sent out everywhere to gather his possessions, which he could arrange for his living by his own spontaneous and free direction. For this reason, the man of God Dunstan, like other guardians of royal treasures, went; so that he might bring back to the king those things he had kept for the purpose of guarding. And when, after some days, he was returning by the same way he had come, laden with the wealth of his possessions, a voice was sent from heaven, saying to him: "Behold, now King Eadred has died in peace." At this voice, the horse on which the man of God was riding suddenly fell dead, because it could not endure the presence of the angelic sublimity. And when he arrived, he found the king at the same time at which the angel had announced to him on his journey, having ended in the supreme death: whose departed spirit the standing throngs of the faithful, likewise the lifeless limbs, as is the custom of mortals, committed to the Creator Lord under the rest of peace.

21. After him, Eadwig arose, the son of King Edmund, indeed young in age, and possessing little wisdom for ruling, although he filled the names of both peoples of kings. To him, a certain woman of high birth, yet foolish, with her adult daughter, clung through a nefarious familiarity, seeking to associate herself and even her daughter under the title of marriage: whom he, as they say, alternately, which now it shames to say, treated with base fondling and without shame of either. And when, at the appointed time, he was anointed and consecrated king by the common election of all the princes of the Angles, on the same day after the royal anointing of sacred institution, he suddenly leapt forth, wanton, leaving joyful feasts or the audible gatherings of his nobles, to the aforementioned lascivious fondling. And when the highest pontiff Odo saw the king's wantonness, especially

on the day of his consecration, displeasing to the confident senate all around, he said to his fellow bishops and the other princes: "Let each of you go, I pray, to bring back the king, so that he may be a pleasant companion in this royal banquet, as befits his satellites." But they, fearing to incur the king's annoyance or the complaints of women, began to withdraw one by one and refused. Finally, they chose from all two whom they knew to be most steadfast in spirit, namely Dunstan the abbot, and Cynegius the bishop, a relative of Dunstan, to bring back the king, willing or unwilling, to the remaining seat. And entering according to the commands of their princes, they found the royal crown, which shone with a marvelous metal of gold or silver and the varied brightness of gems, carelessly torn from the head to the ground, and the king himself, in a malign manner, rolling about as if in a vile pigsty. And they said: "Our nobles have sent us to you, asking that you quickly return to the worthy dining hall of your session, and do not despise joining in the joyful banquets of your nobles." But Dunstan first rebuking the foolishness of the women, with his own hand, while he did not want to rise for him, dragged him from the adulterous bed of the women; and having placed the diadem upon him, he led him with him, although he was seized by the women, to the royal company.

22. Then the same Aedelgyw, such was the name of the infamous woman, twisted her empty eye sockets against the venerable abbot with fervent fury, saying that such a man was beyond measure magnanimous, who would dare to enter the king's secret. For we have heard in the writings of ancient kings that Jezebel, filled with the error of paganism and the venom of a serpent, raged day and night with bitter detestation against the prophets of God and did not cease to pursue them to death: so this shameless woman, from that day forth, filled with the same poisonous breath of Jezebel, although she used a Christian name unworthy, did not cease to persecute the man of God, Dunstan, with hostile counsels, until she fulfilled the pestilential will of her curse with increased enmity against the king. Then, with the con-

sent of the aforementioned king, she subjected all the honor of that order and all the substance of her belongings to her own laws; moreover, under the compulsion of the king's command, she quickly proscribed him to the calamity of exile. For the madness of this raging woman was not so much to be regarded, but rather the more astonishing secret machinations of the disciples, whom he was nurturing to be imbued with sweet doctrine: for they themselves were conspirators under the hidden deceit, who, if they could have detested her wicked losses, should have done so. And while her ejectors looked to register all ecclesiastical matters, behold, from the western part of the temple, the harsh voice of a laughing devil was heard, as if it were the voice of a clapping maid. To whom the man of God, perceiving in his mind who it was, said: "Do not, O enemy, rejoice so much; for as much as you now rejoice in my retreat, so much will you again be saddened in the coming, condemned by God."

23. However, whoever among his friends received this same man of God, cast out by the unjust judgment of the accusing woman, out of love or compassion, gravely incurred the wrath of the king: and therefore he was forced to navigate through the insane waves of the troubled sea and to approach the uncertain exiles of Gaul. And when he had entered the sea as if three miles with the sails unfurled, messengers came from the wicked woman, as they say, who would have plucked out his eyes if he had been found on those shores of the sea. However, he, crossing the watery paths of the blue bridge with swift course, came to an unknown region of the aforementioned Gaul, of which he was almost ignorant of the language and customs. But, accompanied by the mercy of his God, he found favor before a certain prince of that land, who kept him under the paternal affection of charity during the time of his exile. Thus, although he was kindly nurtured daily under the care of the same prince, he remained with a constant mind in the homeland, from which he had been removed without the judgment of piety. He also often let forth a plentiful

stream of tears from his flowing eyes, whenever he considered in exile how great a height of religion he had left in the monastery. Also, long in the meditation of a sorrowful heart, while he contemplated such matters, behold, one night he saw in a most notable vision while sleeping, that which he had been eagerly seeking while awake; this only, as was customary, would have been in the monastery along with the standing crowd of brothers, while the evening praises were being sung.

23. However, whoever among the friends, after these events, received this same man of God, cast out by the unjust judgment of a slanderous woman, into their hospitality out of love or compassion, incurred the king's wrath severely: and for this reason he was forced to navigate the insane waves of the turbulent sea and to approach the uncertain exiles of Gaul. And when he had sailed about three miles into the sea, messengers came from the wicked queen, as they say, who would have plucked out his eyes if he had been found on those shores. But he, crossing the watery ways of the blue sea with rapid course, came to an unknown region of the aforementioned Gaul, whose language and customs he scarcely knew. Yet, accompanied by the mercy of his God, he found favor before a certain prince of that land, who kept him with a paternal affection during his time of exile. Therefore, although he was kindly nurtured daily under the care of the same prince, his mind remained continually in the homeland from which he had been removed without the judgment of piety. He also often shed abundant tears from the flowing eyes, groaning as he remembered how great a height of religion he had left behind in the monastery. Even for a long time, while he meditated with a sorrowful heart on such matters, behold, one night, he saw in a well-known vision while sleeping what he had longed for in his waking mind; this only, that as was usual in the monastery, along with a crowd of standing brothers, while they were singing the evening praises, after the last song "My soul magnifies the Lord," they sang this antiphon: "Why have you slandered the words of truth: you compose words to rebuke: and you

strive to overthrow your friend? Nevertheless [...]," at this point, all seemed to cease singing altogether, nor could they finish it in any way with words or voice, although they brought it back to the same place by singing it repeatedly with futile effort; and they would not admit two neighboring words to be sung together. But he, rebuking them through the same vision, said: "Why do you not want to say to finish the antiphon: 'What you have thought, fulfill it.'" Soon he perceived a divine response from the other side under this voice: "Therefore, I say, because they will never fulfill what they devise in their minds: so that they may also tear you away from the power of this monastery." And awakening after the vision, he gave thanks to the Most High for comforting him. For it was evident from this most certain revelation that, as we have previously mentioned in any words, some of their secret persecutors were present.

5

CHAPTER FIVE

The Bishopric of Worcester and London: then the Archbishopic of Canterbury. The Roman Journey.

24. It happened that the aforementioned king was utterly abandoned by the people of Bruma in the past years, because he had acted foolishly in the committed governance, dispersing the shrewd or wise out of hatred of vanity, and drawing in ignorant ones similar to himself with a zeal for love. After this, thus abandoned by the conspiracy of all, they chose for themselves, as God directed, Edgar, the brother of the same Edward, as king, who would justly strike the unjust with the imperial rod, but would peacefully guard the benign under the same rod of equity. And so, with the whole people as witness, the public matter of kings was separated from the definition of the wise, so that the famous river Thames would delineate the kingdom of both. Then Edgar, having been chosen by the aforementioned people to the kingdom, sent by the nod of God to recall the venerable abbot from the hated exile in which he had been living: not forgetful of how great reverence had been shown to his predecessors, to whom he had paid an unceasing faithful service with salvific counsel: whom, having been brought back from his residence, he honored with all the dignity deserving of him. Meanwhile, the brother of the same Edgar, because he

had deviated from the just judgments of God, expired in a miserable death with his last breath: and he himself, as a rightful heir elected by both peoples, received his kingdom, uniting the divided rights of the kingdoms under one scepter. He again restored B. Dunstan to the honor of his former dignity, as well as his ancestor and several others, whom his brother, previously established in the same elevation, had ordered to be plundered by an unjust judgment.

25. Afterwards, a great assembly of the wise was held in a place called Bradanfoort, and in that place, Dunstan was appointed bishop by the election of all, particularly because he had continually been present at the royal court due to his wise counsel. And while the king, instructed decently by Blessed Dunstan and other wise men in divine manners, began to suppress the wicked widely, to love the just and modest with a pure heart, to subjugate kings and tyrants to himself, to restore or enrich the ruined churches of God, and to gather crowds serving the praise of the Most High, he guarded the whole region under the royal protection of peace. Then he became the pastor of the Church of Wigoricensis: for Cynewald, having lived out the course of mortal life, succumbed, and Blessed Dunstan, appointed by the king, took on the responsibility of this same Church to be kept under pastoral care: in which he immediately planted the vine of true faith and the palm of justice with diligent cultivation, and sowed the wheat of the Holy Trinity in the hearts of the believers, uprooting the thorns of error: through which, after the end of this present age of good works, they would arrive unharmed at eternal life. Therefore, seeing that the aforementioned king observed that the entrusted Church was being rightly guarded by a vigilant pastor, he committed to him the Church of London, bereaved of a pastor, so that he might prepare a bridge to the high peaks of heaven for the great multitude of that city's people, as well as for the remaining multitude of the East Saxons. He carefully governed these two Churches under the rule of pontifical excellence

through many years, and showed both flocks the way that leads to the true sheepfolds of Christ, both by example and by teaching.

26. But after death eagerly consumed the venerable Oda, the archbishop of the metropolitan city and the ruler of the Church of Christ, having finished him off from Adamic condition with insatiable voracity, Aelfsinus, the pastor of the Wintonians, was counted to that same seat of the high priesthood. He, when he hurried to the city of Rome to request the pallium of the principal mitre, encountered great difficulty from the snow in the Alpine mountains; which had so bound him with the chill of rigor that he was about to perish there, and those accompanying him, having buried the pontiff, returned, announcing with tears that such misfortune had befallen them in the aforementioned mountains. After his completion, they chose Byrhtelm, the overseer of the Dorsetensians, as the highest priest of the holy Church of Dorobernensis: and this man was gentle, modest, humble, and kind, to such an extent that he did not restrain the proud or rebellious under the whip of correction, as he ought to have done. For it is the right of rulers to guard the good well and to encourage them towards better things as much as they can with all their strength; but to rebuke the wicked and rebellious under the harshness of correction, until they turn away from the paths of vanity. Therefore, having learned that the aforementioned pontiff was not at all fulfilling these prescribed rights over the people entrusted to him by becoming gentle; the king ordered him to return by the paths he had come, and to reclaim the dignity left behind. Then he appointed Dunstan, whom he knew to be steadfast, as the highest priest of the aforementioned Church, out of divine respect and the counsel of the wise.

27. Soon he, having received the priesthood, set out on a long journey, which is customary for the highest priests, toward the city of Rome by a prosperous route; and the Lord was a companion on that journey, and did not abandon him as he returned in pure faith, as He

Himself promised through the Prophet to any faithful one, saying: I will give you understanding, and I will instruct you in this way you shall go; I will fix my eyes upon you (Ps. XXXI, 8). And again: I will go before you, and I will humble the glorious ones of the earth (Isa. XLV, 2). And when he had made the long journey in haste, and all the provisions, whether carried by horse or by other means, had been entirely expended by his own or others' hands, he said to his steward: What do you have for our sustenance for this night? But he, grumbling, replied, saying: Absolutely nothing; because you cared for nothing to reserve for yourself, while whatever food we seemed to have, you had distributed by your own or external command. And the bishop said to him: Do not be too troubled about this; for our Lord Jesus Christ is sufficiently generous and rich toward all who believe in Him. But he again said: Now, you will see what your Christ will give you for sustenance during this night. And the pontiff arose, for the evening time was approaching, to fulfill the appropriate evening praises in remote places. Yet the aforementioned steward still shouted with foolish murmuring, saying: Go ahead and worship only your Christ, not attending to anything else we need. For there were in that same village, where the man of God was then lodging with his companions, messengers of a certain venerable abbot, who were waiting for three days for the blessed arrival of the pontiff: and they came before he could complete the evening praises with singing, with rich gifts of gratitude, and with all the delights of that region, greeting the bishop with love from the mouth of the abbot and the faithful band of his brothers. He, gladly receiving those charitable blessings, greeted the gracious abbot, along with the devoted company of the brothers who were staying with him. Afterwards, indeed, from those same gifts, aided by the charity of the aforementioned brothers, they lived delightfully for a long time: and the foolish murmuring of the insolent steward, firmly overcome by the faith of the pontiff, ceased.

28. Then, led by the Lord, he arrived at the desired Church of the Roman See, where he gloriously received the principal pallium under the privilege of the episcopate, along with the apostolic blessing; and after visiting the shrines of the saints and comforting the poor of Christ, he returned home through the paths of peace. And when the supreme pontiff of the Angles arrived, affected by spiritual charisma, he began first to subject himself, as higher than the other orders of priests, to the higher services of Christ; lest, while he ministered the nourishment of true faith to others or pointed out the straight path to heaven with the saving word, he himself (as the Apostle says) should become reprobate (1 Cor. IX, 27) and contrary to his own preaching. Then he aimed to renew what was destroyed, to justify what was neglected, to enrich the holy places, to love the righteous, to recall the erring to the way, to build the churches of God, and to fulfill the name of the true shepherd in all things.

29. Indeed, if I were to emit a thousand sounds with a iron tongue against nature day and night, I could not possibly express all the beneficial works of his virtues, which he performed either openly or even secretly. However, I profess that I can relate one thing about him, that although he dwelt here in a fleshly veil, yet in mind, whether he was awake or resting in sleep, he always remained in the heavens, as the Apostle Paul said: Our conversation is in heaven (Phil. III, 20). This was certainly often evident when he dictated the divine hymns of the sacred, which he never received from men, but had learned through a receptive understanding from the blessed citizens of the heavenly realm by divine revelation, as the following sentence makes clear. One night, after pious prayers and after the last office of Compline, while he had given his blessed limbs to rest, he saw with certain demonstration how his own, which he had revealed to this world, was being joined in marriage to a certain powerful king as a bride, under the testimony of the highest of his princes and under the title of a dowry; and that there would be such joy among the singers at this

royal wedding that the entire joyful multitude would sound the sweetest hymn in honor of the king. And while these things were being carried out for a long time, a certain youth, clothed in snowy whiteness, approached among the voices of the singers, saying to the pontiff in that very vision: Do you not see and hear how this entire rejoicing multitude glorifies the great king by resounding in their ranks, while you alone remain silent? Why do you not resound with us in the worthy praises of such a king, who should especially rejoice in such a union of a parent? Then he replied that he did not know such songs and was entirely ignorant of what they were singing in praise of the king. But he said: Do you wish me to instruct you what you ought to sing? And while he professed with humble demeanor that he wanted to teach him, he soon imbued him with this model of the antiphon: O King of the nations, ruler of all, grant us mercy because of the seat of your majesty, King Christ, of sinners. Alleluia. Indeed, this was often repeated and well established in the same vision, he emitted a murmuring sound upon waking; but immediately he ordered it to be written in memory of letters, before it could be forgotten, and commanded a certain monk to learn it freshly: and at dawn he made all those subject to him, both monks and clerics, to sound this by learning: he himself always singing among the voices of those who were modulating with an excessive shower of tears: Truly he is not false, who showed me this sonorous antiphon in the vision of this night. Hence, without a doubt (as we have already said above), it became clear in which parts of the places, while his body rested, his spirit happily remained in the meantime.

30. Now I would like, before I hurriedly proceed further by reading, to have an expert interpreter to explain to me the mystery of this wondrous vision: or, if I could manage with some effort, to provide the interpretation myself as best as I can, although it may be melted down like warm fire. For I indeed think that the mother of the holy pontiff, joined in marriage to a great king, signifies the holy Church, which

has regenerated him or many others in a motherly manner through the spiritual womb of sacred baptism from the privilege of the first parent. Indeed, she who now seems to adhere to the highest King, namely, Christ the Lord, through the acknowledgment of true faith, and through the embrace of divine love, as a bride joined to her husband, this same holy mother Church cries out in the Song of Songs: "The king has brought me into his chamber; we will rejoice and be glad in you, remembering your breasts above wine; the upright love you" (Song of Solomon I, 3). And again: "The king has brought me into his wine cellar; he has set love in me; sustain me with flowers, comfort me with apples, for I am lovesick. His left hand is under my head, and his right hand embraces me" (Song of Solomon II, 4-6), etc. However, I assert that the mother of the same holy pontiff, joined in marriage to the exalted king, can signify the Church of his own episcopate, which had been entrusted to be kept in the stead of the eternal King, namely Christ and the Lord, and to console with the pure integrity of virginity, so that the same Lord, crucified on the gibbet for the sins of the people, entrusted his mother, the Virgin, to the disciple, saying: "Behold, I commit to you my Mother." The military ranks also, exulting in songs of praise to their king, are the citizens of the angels above, who, although at one time they were enemies of men due to the discordant distance of sins, I do not doubt; now, however, since they see the inhabitants of both heaven and earth united in one family of the Father, they do not cease day and night to sing such songs to the true King God: "Praise our God, all his saints, and you who fear him, small and great, for the Lord God omnipotent reigns in heaven, as well as on earth; and therefore let us rejoice and be glad and give glory to him" (Revelation XIX, 5). This same glory, the multitude of the heavenly army sings to the newborn Lord, announcing peace on earth to men of good will (Luke II, 14). Indeed, this peace, which the blessed Apostle requested, saying: "He is our peace, who made both one" (Ephesians II, 14), etc. For when he saw the youth clothed in shining white garments, partly rebuking himself for being silent about the praise of the aforementioned prince; I do not doubt that he is his guardian angel, who, by instructing him with spiritual words, warned him not to allow the silence of a mute dog (to imitate), permitting the hidden enemy, namely the devil, to stealthily seize the souls of those entrusted to him, or the talent of his God: but that he should openly proclaim and with a pious confession of heart declare that Christ is the king and ruler of all, of the heavenly, earthly, and infernal; and that he should intercede for them on account of the throne and name of his majesty, first for his own, then for the sins of the people, imploring that he might be a merciful pardoner of sins, for which he did not hesitate to offer himself once at the command of the fatherly parent.

6

CHAPTER SIX

Various visions. Preparation for death.

31. By these aforementioned methods, he often learned the melodies of sacred hymns or other praises to God through a vigilant spirit from divine teachings, although his human limbs lay subdued in the sleep of slumber, as it is written in Solomon: "I sleep, but my heart is awake" (Song of Solomon V, 2). And again the prophet Isaiah says: "In the night my spirit watches for you, O Lord, for your commandments are my light" (Isaiah XXVI, 9). Who, even while placed in the world, clearly saw the enemies of the human race with his eye, as it was declared at the imminent and miserable death of King Edmund. Therefore, while this king was accustomed to entertain in the usual manner with his own dignities, it happened that Blessed Dunstan, still the abbot of this king, was present at the gathering, being near to a certain primary duke, namely Elfstane, on the way to the nearest castle, and being a fellow horseman. And behold, suddenly looking ahead on the path of progression, he saw among the royal trumpeters a horrendous enemy playing about. When he had gazed at him for a long time in astonishment, he said to the aforementioned primary companion: "Do you think, my dear, that you can see what I see?" But he replied: "I see nothing except what I ought to see." And he said: "Then

mark your own eyes with the healing seal of the holy cross, and prove if you can see what I see." And when, at the command of the blessed Father Dunstan, he marked his eyes with a light impression of the holy cross, he immediately saw, as a testimony of such a great man, the same enemy of God and men, appearing in the form of a certain little black man; and soon, from the demonstration of the nefarious demon, he was able to perceive some misfortunes of value that were about to come upon some of them; and having made the sign of the cross, the enemy disappeared.

32. After they had ceased to speak of this wicked apparition of the deceptive vision, the aforementioned prince asked the already mentioned man of God to explain to him the dreams of his vision recently revealed. For he said that he had seen the aforementioned king with his princes and all the nobility, as was customary, sitting in the dining hall of his palace; and among the joyful banquets of the ministers and entertainers, the same king whom I mentioned had fallen asleep in slumber: and after the heavy burden of his sleep, almost all his princes or wise men had changed into the forms of goats and sheep, leaving behind their human shapes. To this, B. Dunstan immediately replied with prophetic eloquence, saying: The king's sleep is a sign of his death; and that you saw the magnates or wise men of his transformed into mute animals or insensate beings indicates a future time, in which almost all the princes of this region and the rulers of affairs will, by their own free will, deviate from the path of truth, of which they are wise, like foolish animals without a shepherd.

33. Thus having taken place, they arrived at the royal village, always conversing about these matters. And when the twilight of that day came, the man of God Dunstan saw again at the evening banquet of the king the same or some other enemy lurking among the many ministers. Then, if I am not mistaken, after three days, on the very day when the aforementioned king was to perish by iron; he saw for the

third time a certain unknown man, I do not know whether an enemy or even a spiritual man, carrying a large scroll of paper in his hand, densely written at the tips, at the very moment when the king, after the celebration of the masses, was returning to the hall for his last banquet. When he asked who he was, he replied in Saxon that he was from the eastern kingdom and that he had certain secret nuptial words with the king. While he was being announced to the king and was to be introduced into his presence as was customary for those who come, he did not appear anywhere: but on that very day, alas! as I said, the bitter harshness of a cruel death stealthily entered the innermost parts of his heart through the dagger of a treacherous thief. Behold how quickly the predictions concerning the king became clear to the blessed man. As for the princes, they were not revealed except in the times of King Eadwig, if a king can rightly be called one who neither governed himself nor others well. For indeed, B. Father Dunstan was led by the spirit of God, as the Apostle says (Rom. VIII, 14), therefore he had deserved such mysteries as a son of God: to such an extent that many asserted he was uttering the most vain deliriums of words, while he prophesied many things through the prophetic mouth and the inspiration of the Holy Spirit, which we afterward saw accomplished with the most evident signs.

34. Here he also saw and heard without any difficulty certain wonders of spiritual secrets, which I now weave into mysteries. For he was a venerable man, always inflamed with the love of God, and for this reason he diligently visited the places of holy monasteries for the edification of souls. He also came from this healthful custom to the place of the baths, where hot water bubbles up dripping from the hiding places of the abyss, which the inhabitants have been accustomed to call Bath in their native tongue. And when he had been kindly received there by the brothers of that place, he saw after the hour of dinner the soul of a certain scholar from the monastery of Glastonbury, being carried to the heights of heaven by the angels of God with hymns of praise,

and surrounded by the great funerals of the heavenly citizens. However, the next day, as a testimony to this wondrous vision, a certain prior from the aforementioned monastery, named Ceolwyus, wishing to discuss the monastic matters and causes of his brothers with the bishop as was customary, came. As soon as he had given his blessing to him coming from the monastery, he eagerly asked if all was well with his brothers: and he, not foreseeing the death of the boy at all, replied that everything had been established in the safety of integrity. But he, with a modest discourse, since he had been much clearer about his own vision than that: "I do not think," he said, "that all will be well with all in human excesses." And he: "Indeed, all is well, except that the little boy of our community underwent inevitable death yesterday at noon." "This is," said the holy bishop, "what I said. May his blessed spirit rest in peace according to our vision."

35. Again, while he was dwelling in his own monastery, that is, Glastonbury, the same vigilant overseer of Christ's sheep was walking with one of the monks of the same monastery, from house to house, considering the fodder of the brothers or other necessities of the same. And while returning, having seen the supplies, he came to the western climates of the ancient Church, he heard from afar a voice sent from heaven unexpectedly, which had invited the monk walking with him to heavenly delights with sweet words, saying: "Come, come, Aelfsige, come:" for this was, I believe, the name of that brother. Then the blessed man, understanding the advocacy of his merit client, said: "Therefore, hasten strongly, brother, to prepare yourself as soon as possible; for in the very near days, called by the Lord, you will migrate from the filth of this world to Him." Indeed, within not many days, this was fulfilled concerning him, as he had predicted, by a probable indication. From there, in the same place, he ordered a church with square corners to be built in the manner of a fan, and he honorably consecrated it in honor of the blessed John the Baptist. O great merit

of the glorious prelate, who deserved to see visions of angels while alive and to hear their wonderful voices!

36. Therefore, while he was staying in the city of his own episcopate, it was part of his holy custom, among other pursuits of elevation, to frequently visit the holy places during the secret hours of the night, due to the multitude of people coming to him, or even due to the occupations of many others, by always chanting the holy psalmody. And he came, bound by this law of religion, to the chapel of the blessed Father Augustine, intending to pray during the night, as I said; and while he was supplying sacred prayers there, he proceeded to the eastern church of the Mother of God, to pray just as much. And when he had approached and arrived at this place, singing, he unexpectedly heard unusual sounds of voices, resounding with a subtle melody in this same basilica. He then immediately looked through a certain opening and saw that the mentioned church was filled with brilliant light, and the virgin choirs in the choir were singing this hymn of the poet Sedulius, chanting: "Let us sing, companions, to the Lord," etc. Moreover, he perceived that they were responding to each verse in a reciprocal voice, as if in a concert of their own circling, first resounding the first line of the same hymn like human virgins, saying: "Let us sing, companions, to the Lord, let us sing honor: Sweet love of Christ may resound from a pious mouth," etc. These, I say, are the venerable signs of spiritual gifts, and countless other things, which neither I nor anyone else dwelling in this life can adequately narrate with any human eloquence; the distinguished prelate Dunstan, because he walked in the ways of righteousness, deserved to receive.

37. Now therefore, since I cannot explain all the exercises of his good deeds, even if I were to dwell on them day and night in the utmost sagacity of meditation, deprived of natural sleep; yet I deem it fair to at least relate those things which either I myself have seen or heard, stimulated by the just admonition of God, to the best of my

ability in charity. For while he laboriously inhabited the tediousness of this life, his utmost zeal was to persistently engage in sacred prayers and in the ten-stringed psalmody of David, either to spend the night overcoming sweet sleep in vigils, or to always labor fervently in ecclesiastical works; or even to correct false writings when he could behold the first light of the day from the east; or to discern true and false among men with keen judgment; or to make all the quarrelsome or discordant peaceful and quiet with gentle speech; or to provide pious assistance to widows, orphans, pilgrims, and strangers in their needs; or to justly separate inept or unjust unions; or to strengthen every human order, arranged in threefold purpose, with the word of life or example; or to support the churches of God, to enrich them with pleasing righteousness from the just assessment of his own acquisition; or even to instruct the unlearned of both orders, whether men or women, whom he could season day and night with heavenly salt, that is, with the teaching of saving wisdom. Therefore, all this English land is filled with his holy teaching, shining before God and men, like the sun and the moon; or even when he deemed it appropriate to fulfill the due hours of his servitude and the other celebrations of the Mass for Christ the Lord, he exercised them with such integrity of mind in chanting that he seemed to speak face to face with the Lord himself; although previously he had been too much entangled in the conflicts of a tumultuous people; meanwhile, with his eyes and hands always directed to heaven in the manner of St. Martin, never relaxing his spirit from prayer. Whenever he performed any other work worthy of perfection or even praise, even in the sacred ordinations of priests, the consecrations of churches or altars, or even in any institutions of divine matters, he always completed this with an excessive shower of tears, which the invisible holy inhabitant, the Holy Spirit, who continually dwelt in him, powerfully elicited from the streams of his eyes.

38. And when the heavenly inspector beheld all these pious endeavors of the blessed man with the longest contemplation, he finally de-

cided to grant a more merciful end to his laborious struggles, so that he might receive in heaven the reward for which he had often toiled, while he bore the light burden of it on earth. For the day of the Ascension of our Lord God was approaching, the day of his advocacy, on which day, however, he had completed the solemn Masses without any injury, as directed by the Lord, and had ministered the last nourishment of the word of God to the people entrusted to him with many showers of tears; always teaching that the Son of God descended from the highest seats of heaven for the salvation of humanity, to reveal through his piety that he and his Father, together with the Holy Spirit, are one God; and that on the same day, having defeated the devil and liberated his people, he would ascend to the heavens from which he seemed to come. When he had concluded this exhortation, he, with excessive love of heart, requested what he had originally sought with swift petition, namely, that the Almighty Lord, by paternal mercy, would grant the faithful, namely, the members of Jesus Christ, the ability to ascend, since Christ, the beginning and head of all, had powerfully ascended on the aforementioned day. With these words and other wholesome admonitions, he fervently encouraged the hearts of those entrusted to him three times during the celebration of that day: first, as the ecclesiastical order rightly indicates after the reading of the Gospel; secondly, after the blessing of the power conferred upon him; and thirdly, after the conference of pious peace, when we sang in common: "Lamb of God, who takes away the sins of the world, have mercy on us," at which time he himself desired the lambs entrusted to him, lightened from the burdens of sin, to be offered piously.

This work was produced in association with:

www.ingramcontent.com/pod-product-compliance
Lightning Source LLC
LaVergne TN
LVHW061623070526
838199LV00078B/7395